W9-DHX-950

Lyle Stuart, Publisher ••⅃S⅃ New York

THIS IS
WHAT WE
FOUND

BY RALPH AND CARL CREGER

THIS IS WHAT WE FOUND

Queries regarding rights and permissions should
be addressed to Lyle Stuart at 225 Lafayette Street,
New York 12, New York

Typography by The Polyglot Press

Edited by Eileen Brand
Designed by Barbara Bert

Printed in the United States of America

DEDICATION

In the vortex of Little Rock, many of us have questioned. A number of us have changed. Some of us have matured.

We have learned. We have learned from our experiences. We have learned from our teachers.

Since 1957, school teachers in Little Rock, Arkansas, have been subjected to pressures above and beyond those generally known by teachers elsewhere. Their refusal to bow to these pressures may have been the key to the preservation of the public school system in the South.

These teachers did not advocate segregation, nor integration. They tried to carry on the process of education. Like most educators, they valued freedom of thought and opinion. Thanks to them, and others like them, there have been no book burnings in Little Rock.

Most teachers made it clear that they expected to see a display of good citizenship as the schools were integrated.

Many of these instructors paid a high price for doing what they felt was right, and for speaking out against what they often believed to be sheer demagoguery on the part of state leaders. They came to know the anonymous telephone call at midnight, and the threatening anonymous letter.

Those who are far removed from the scene probably do not realize how near we came to closing our public schools in the fall of 1959, and how the refusal to close them affected the entire South. The reason they did not close was due primarily to a gallant group of public school teachers here in Little Rock who refused to bow to intense pressure by the extremist groups and pressure from the Governor.

Part of the Little Rock School Board, with the support of Gov-

5

ernor Faubus, tried to dismiss fifty of these teachers in the summer of 1959. No reasons were given for these dismissals, other than the vague hint that some of those "purged" had been "soft" on integration. Three of the Board members refused to be a party to this wholesale "firing" of teachers. As a result, a special school board election was held.

When the people of Little Rock finally saw the fruits of demagoguery in the wholesale firing of many respected school teachers, they at last roused themselves and did something about it. The extreme segregationists were replaced with men pledged to preserve the public schools.

This special election may have been the turning point for public schooling throughout an entire region.

There were turmoil and ferment in Little Rock as this election was held. Its issues forced some of us to reexamine old notions and ancient prejudices with fresh, clear vision.

Shortly after the election, in November, 1959, a history instructor in Central High School required his students to prepare a composition on any subject pertaining to American history.

What follows is the result of this classroom assignment.*

We respectfully dedicate this book to the public school teachers in Little Rock, Arkansas.

—Ralph and Carl Creger
Little Rock, Arkansas, 1960

* *This Is What We Found* began as a history assignment for Carl Creger, a seventeen-year-old white student of Little Rock's Central High School. Ralph Creger is his father, chief train dispatcher in Little Rock for the Rock Island Railroad. Both father and son became so interested in the topic that they collaborated to expand it to its present length. It wound up as both a study of the history of the American Negro and the reasons why a white son and father in Little Rock came to champion equal rights and opportunities for Negroes.—Ed.

WHERE
WE
BEGAN

As a father and son directly affected by the integration turmoil surrounding Central High School in Little Rock, Arkansas, in September, 1957, we were disturbed by what seemed to us a lack of Christian principles in many of our fellow citizens. We were shocked by the willingness of some men in high political office to exploit an emotional crisis for political gain.

We felt that anything causing such tension, ill will and bitterness as we had witnessed justified as much study and research as we could find time for. We saw that we had no right to blindly accept the theories advanced by so many in our community—particularly of the older generation.

We read nearly every book pertaining to race or related matters offered by the Public Library. In addition, we tried to make an objective study of the Scriptures.

In studying the Scriptures, we found nothing to indicate that the Negro should be set apart. Rather, we found that the Scriptural references generally quoted by racists actually referred to the godly versus the ungodly, wherever separation of peoples was urged.

Acts VIII, 27-31, tells of Phillip's experience with the Ethiopian:

And he arose and went: and, behold, a man of Ethiopia, a eunuch of great authority under Candace, queen of the Ethiopians, who had the charge of all her treasure, and had come to Jerusalem for to worship. Was returning, and sitting in his chariot read Esaias the Prophet. Then the Spirit said unto Phillip, Go near, and join thyself to this chariot. And Phillip ran thither to *him*, and heard him read the prophet Esaias; and said, Understandeth thou what thou readest? And he said, How can I, except some man should guide me? And he desired Phillip that he would come up and sit with him.

What a wonderful opening this would have provided for the Lord (if He had wanted) to have explained to us that the Ethiopians were really a simple people, not to be trusted, unlearned and unable to assume leadership. It is obvious that such was not the case. The man was everything the racist tells us the Negro is not. He was a man of learning. He was trustworthy. He was a man of great authority.

Verses such as these may or may not be significant; but certainly we found nothing in the Bible to indicate that the Ethiopians were either more or less worthy than others, or that they were inclined toward stupidity, immorality, dishonesty, crimes of violence or *any* of the undesirable characteristics attributed to the Negro by the racists, and which the racist claims are innate.

On the positive side, there seems to be a clear message to men of all races in the Golden Rule:

Do unto others as you would have them do unto you.

ANCIENT NEGRO CULTURES

Our story is basically the history of the Negro in America; but we may better understand the subject from some of the background of the Negro peoples, before their arrival on this continent.

In presenting this praiseworthy (though frequently tragic) history, emphasis will be placed on conditions as they were, and are today, rather than as some might wish to believe them to be.

There are those to whom race is all important, and to whom racial supremacy has become a religion. These people frequently declare that the colored races have contributed little that is worthwhile to the civilization of the world. They say that the colored people, even though inhabiting areas rich in natural resources, have not exploited these resources as they might have. These racists always fail to mention that climatic conditions between the Tropic of Cancer and the Tropic of Capricorn are not as conducive to the energy and drive needed to industrialize as those of the temperate zones.

Be that as it may, the idea that the darker-skinned peoples have traditionally been culturally and industrially inferior simply will not stand up under the careful study of history and science. It is not often called to our attention, but students of history generally agree that, for several centuries before Christ, Ethiopia, Egypt and other African countries had a high degree of culture and industry when our forebears in Western Europe were existing in a state of savagery. Nations such as

China, Babylonia, Greece and others of varied racial groups have had their periods of glory.

Why the western European nations and America have been in the dominant position in recent centuries is a matter of conjecture and one guess is probably as good as another. Possibly it is because the Christian religion was taken first to these nations, as it spread up through Greece and Rome, then to Western Europe and on to America. This, of course, is only an opinion; but it seems obvious that the so-called "Christian" nations have prospered and have gained the highest attainments in culture, science and industry in recent centuries.

Prior to the time of Christ, however, it was Negro peoples who founded the civilizations along the Ganges, the Euphrates and the Nile. Early Babylonia was founded by a Negro race. The Assyrians showed a distinct Negroid strain, and early Egypt was predominantly Negro. These cultures were crude and primitive by today's standards, but they represented the highest attainment of mankind after thousands of years of unawakened savagery. (1)

The Negroes were not a single people. They came from tribes as different as the several nations of Europe. They were later captured from provinces covering large parts of Central and Western Africa. Among them were the Moors from the Northwesterly coast, tribesmen from equatorial regions, peoples of the Cameroons, the Congo and vast stretches of the Niger Valley and the tall blacks from the Gold Coast. (2)

Contrary to popular belief, many of the African tribes were far above barbarism. Settled farming, exchange of goods and the use of money, organized governments, elaborate religious forms, beautiful arts and crafts were common over the wide area of Guinea, from which most of American slaves were to come.

In describing the upper regions of the Senegal River, André Brue of the French African Company in the eighteenth century wrote:

"The farther you go to the sea, the country on the river seems more fruitful and well improved; abounding with Indian corn, pulse, fruit, etc. . . . Their smiths particularly work neatly in gold and silver and make knives, hatchets, reaping hoods, spades and shares to cut iron. Their potters make pots to boil their food. Weaving is their principal trade."

Another author reported: "Along the banks of the Senegal were found kingdoms with highly developed arts and with vast meadows which feed large herds of cattle, with poultry numerous." (3)

A large number of archaeologists today believe the Negro was the only user of iron among primitive people. It appears that, at a time when Europeans were still satisfied with crude stone tools, the African had invented or adopted the art of smelting iron. Karl Andree declares the Negro developed his own iron kingdoms; Georg August Schweinfurth, Felix Von Luschan, Franz Boas and others incline to the belief that the Negroes invented the smelting of iron and passed it on to the Egyptians and to modern Europe. (4)

Neither ancient Europe, Western Asia nor China knew iron; and everything points to its introduction in Africa.

Long before cotton weaving was a British industry, the Sudan supplied a large part of the world with cotton cloth.

Among the forest farmers in Africa, the village was

the center of life. The Negroes among all the great groups of the natural races, seemed to excel as tillers of the ground. Some despised agriculture and bred cattle, but others combined both occupations.

Probably the first Negro to see the new world was Pedro Alonzo, Captain of the Niña, who sailed with Columbus. Negroes accompanied Balboa when he discovered the Pacific. They were with Cortez in Mexico and Coronado in New Mexico. Estevanico, a Negro, with De Vaca discovered the Zuñi Indians. However, Negroes did not arrive in America in large numbers until they came as slaves. (5)

SLAVERY IN AMERICA

Slavery certainly did not originate in America, nor with the Negro. Man had enslaved his fellowman for many centuries prior to the discovery of America, and even prior to the birth of Christ. Ancient history is filled with accounts of human bondage. The Jews were slaves for four hundred years until Moses led them out of Egypt; and, even then, many of the Jewish people had become so accustomed to slavery that they would have preferred to remain in slavery to taking the risk of attempting to escape.

The Romans made slaves of the people of Greece. It was not uncommon for a Roman to have as his personal slave a Greek who was far superior to him culturally and intellectually; but, as Rome was the superior power, the Greeks were helpless.

Fifty years before the discovery of America, Negro slaves from Africa were imported to Europe. This was started by the Portuguese as incident to their commercial expansion. In 1444, a group of Portuguese adventurers, known as the Company of Lagos, captured more than a hundred and fifty Negro men, women and children from the islands of Nar and Tidar.

These slaves were described as a recompense from God for the labor the Portuguese had given in his service. These were landed at Lagos and Prince Henry himself was there to receive them in the name of Christ and to claim his share. This was the beginning of the modern slave trade with Africa and the beginning also of its justification on the grounds of winning souls for Christ.

Cheap labor was one of the most pressing needs in America in the seventeenth and eighteenth centuries. Forests had to be cleared, houses built, crops planted and harvested. At first, this need was met by the use of indentured servants from Europe; but they proved unsatisfactory, for two reasons. First, as soon as they had repaid their indebtedness, they were free and of no more value to their master. Secondly, since they looked like their masters, they could escape to another locality with little chance of being apprehended.

The introduction of the Negro slave solved both these problems; and by 1715 there were approximately sixty thousand Negro slaves in the American colonies. By the period of the Revolution, this number had increased to five hundred thousand.

They came in chains from everywhere along the west coast of Africa, the Gold, the Ivory, and the Grain Coasts, and from thousands of nameless villages inland. They were people of at least four great sub-races, the Negritians, the Fellatahs, the Bantus and the Gallas, and many tribes such as the Kaffirs, Senegalese and the Mandingos.

The plains and valleys of Africa rang with their cries. Chained to each other, neck and foot, under the merciless sun and the whine of the slavers' whips, these terrified Negroes were marched to the coast. Two out of five died on these marches, with the worst yet to come.

Most of the slaves arrived at such West Indian isles as Haiti. As stated, a large percentage of slaves died on the journey from their homes to the coast of Africa, and another third of them died on the voyages to America. Those who reached Haiti prospered, though strictly by comparison. The Spanish were notorious for maiming slaves for small offenses. The French developed refinements of punishment that included hamstringing, branding and merciless floggings.

Insurrection, if discovered, resulted in death so slow and tortured as to make the most depraved sadist blush; and, if only a few suffered this type of punishment, many more suffered and died from a combination of overwork and a diet of rotten fish.

Slaves often worked eighteen hours a day. Men and women alike went to the fields at daybreak and drudged until dark; or at midnight they went to the boiling house where cane was rendered and worked to the following noon. Deaf and blind with weariness, slaves were sometimes wrenched into the gears of the mills and mangled like so many stalks of cane.

For the individual, of course, there was always self-murder; and this was often resorted to. Many African tribes, such as the Ibo, were noted for their tendency to commit suicide rather than suffer slavery. More resourceful individuals stirred up rebellions, or ran away.

Not all slaves could revolt or run away, and those who did neither, and did not die, remained to be broken in. They then were exported to other islands and to the mainland of America.

The American colonists were at first blind to the potentials of Negro labor. The first black men brought to Virginia were not true slaves, and slavery had no legal status there for forty years. Soon, however, it began to be plain that there were exploitable possibilities in Negro labor far greater than those of white servitude. First, the supply was practically inexhaustible and, perhaps more important, they were visibly different and could easily be apprehended in the event of escape. Because of this visible difference, many slave owners tried to rationalize that the Christian precepts of kindness and humane dealings need not apply to the Negro. Thus began in America the rationalization of race-caste which is still with us to a lesser degree today, especially among those who do not take the trouble to inform themselves properly of the facts.

In New England, as the Puritans pushed inland from the sea, they cut timber and built ships to send their furs and fish to foreign markets. Later, they traded in slaves. Usually their slaves were Indians captured in wars and sold or exchanged to the sugar islands. However, slavery itself did not prove to be successful in New England because of the type of economy there. The soil would not support a plantation-type economy; so they turned to shipbuilding, manufacturing, small businesses and dairying.

The slave in the North was important chiefly as an item of trade. The first American slave ship, the *Desire*, put out from Salem on the Massachusetts coast. She was owned by a company of Puritans.

In contrast to the North, the agricultural economy of the South seemed ideally suited to the use of slaves. So the number of slaves in that area continued to grow.

Almost from the first, there was bloodshed. In Gloucester County, Virginia, in 1663, Negro slaves joined with white indentured servants in a conspiracy to rebel; but the plot was discovered. The ringleaders were drawn and quartered and their bloody heads impaled on posts in a public place. A slave plot to wipe out the whites threw three Virginia counties into a panic in 1687. Again, the leaders were caught and put to death, but this did not deter other slaves in their desperate bids for freedom. By 1710, there had been a dozen revolts attempted or accomplished in Virginia, Maryland, New Jersey and Massachusetts.

Arson was another favorite tool of the rebellious slaves. Many a planter was awakened in the dead of night to find his stable, grain piles, or even his dwelling, in flames. Many instances are recorded of slave insurrections on shipboard and, in some cases, these mutinies were successful and the white crew members were killed and thrown overboard.

The concept of the patient, docile Negro is a historical delusion which has mostly come into being in the past century, after two or three hundred years of brutal treatment and systematic oppression. This concept was in complete contradiction to the law and to the

Black Codes, which said, in effect, that the Negro was restive, dangerous and murderous under slavery. They assumed that the Negro loved freedom enough to risk his life for it on only the dimmest chance of winning, and that, in order to quench the leaping fires of his rebellious nature, the flood of despotism must mount unchecked.

Eventually, most slave-owners realized that they could obtain more desirable results by rewards to their slaves than with brutality and corporal punishment. Nevertheless, there were brutal masters; and almost all overseers felt a few lashes would not be amiss in order to reach the production expected.

Those who chose to be brutal could do so with no fear of punishment. The Negro had no recourse to the courts and his testimony as a witness against a white man was invariably discounted.

There can be no doubt that there were many slaves who felt a real affection for their masters. There were even a few who, upon being freed, voluntarily returned to their masters. But the simple historical record shows that there were many, many more who hated slavery. They were the ones who had the ordinary run of masters and who lived the usual life of a slave. Their shelters were windowless, one-room cabins (which might be no more commodious than a chicken coop) to house a family of seven or eight. The picture of the grey-headed retired slave resting in blissful security outside the cabin door is largely a romantic fiction.

Most planters believed there was more profit in working a slave to death in eight or ten years and then buying another strong replacement than in working him moderately for twenty years. If a slave outlived his usefulness or became crippled or incurably ill, the master, to be rid of his responsibility, usually freed him to become a public charge.

Profit was the slaveholder's motive. On smaller plantations where the work was owner-supervised, slaves were less brutally treated than those handled by overseers; but they worked just as hard. Children were commonly sent to the fields at the age of seven, or earlier. On the large plantations, with twenty-five or more slaves, overseers were used. These overseers had no human interest in the slave even to match the minimum interest of the master. Few questions were asked of the overseer as long as he produced; and production was exacted at the end of a lash or the mouth of a pistol.

Even though slavery had become firmly established in the South, opposition to it continued to mount, particularly in the South. In the early eighteen hundreds, it had reached such proportions that it began to appear likely the problem would be resolved by the voluntary abandonment of slavery. In addition to the opposition to slavery on moral grounds, many were beginning to question the economic wisdom of the system.

But, during this period, the cotton gin was invented and perfected. Cotton became a much more profitable crop than it had been. Slavery, consequently, was much more profitable than it had been; so the abolitionists' voices were silenced, at least in the South.

Past and present, when we think of the Negro, his trials, tribulations and his impact on our society, we think first of the South. A great deal of criticism has been directed at the South from other parts of America.

Not infrequently those quickest to criticize are hardly qualified to do so. Reports of denial of equal rights to Negroes in such places as Deerfield, Illinois, Levittown, Pennsylvania, and Dearborn, Michigan, are fresh in our memory.

Possibly before going further, a quotation from Hodding Carter's book, *Winds of Fear,* might be in order. Carter's book is about a small southern town he calls Carvell City, which is beset by race problems.

It reads as follows:

If you have not lived in Carvell City, it is too easy to denounce its masters, forgetting that they are also slaves of the fear which impels them. If you have lived too long and too casually in Carvell City, it is too easy to accept the inevitability of its ways. A thing then to remember about Carvell City is that hate and suspicion and intolerance are not peculiar to its people. Nor are they innate. Save for the accident of geography and the design of earlier exploiters of our land, the white men and women of Carvell City might be the critics and the men and women of New England the criticized in this tragic predicament of race. (6)

We feel that all of us, both North and South, could get something of value from recognizing the truth of Carter's observation. This truth applies to slavery and to racial problems as we confront them today. Those in the North should not attempt to solve all our race problems until they can put their own house in order. By the same token, we in the South should not attempt to justify injustice and lack of Christian ethics in our own community on the grounds that injustice may also be found elsewhere. All this, of course, is getting away from the continuity of our story, but it has been mentioned because it applies to the Negroes' struggle in the eighteen hundreds, as it does today.

HOW SLAVES REBELLED

All during the years from 1800 to the Civil War, resistance to slavery by slaves continued. Slave rebellions led by such men as Denmark Vesey, Gabriel Prosser and others are well known. More often, slaves escaped singly or in pairs, working their way to the Northern states or to Canada via the "Underground Railroad."

However, the real threat to the efficiency of the slave system lay in those who did not escape, in their day-to-day and hour-to-hour disaffection, in their silent, passive, mocking resistance, the dawdling, the pretending to be dumb, the pretending not to see and hear and understand, pretending to be sick, and in the sudden explosive leap of violence, a slave alone or with others daring to be bold, defiant, murderous and desperate enough to die.

The frequency of suicide among slaves was a real problem for slaveholders. Time and again, slave narratives mention suicide or infanticide. They frequently went together. Slaveholders were not disposed to mention the subject because of the possibility of imitation, but what the planters did not keep quiet about was the slaves' trick of feigning illness. The masters mistook, or preferred to mistake, the dawdling manner, the laggard bearing for laziness and stupidity. But only the knowing master could discover the deception when slaves pretended sickness. Slaves knew of herbs that would pepper them with a rash or induce vomiting and fever.

None of the slave states escaped resistance to slavery. For the slaves, insurrection was a deliberate plunge into a holocaust. Even to conspire toward this end was to take a step that led to the rack, the gallows or the torch; for, no matter how bold and sagacious the leader or how resolute the followers, the rebellions were invariably lost causes. The reasons were not difficult to find. Scattered as slaves were, opportunities for effective planning were few. Masters planted informers and spies; and these betrayers, bribed by promises of rewards or corrupted by selfish hope, were great hazards to success. Therefore, those slaves who were able to escape to the North and educate themselves, make speeches and write of their problems were probably most effective in advancing the cause of freedom.

One of the most famous of those escaping slavery was Frederick Douglass. Born a slave in Maryland about 1817, he was sent, while still young, to work in Baltimore as an errand boy. His mistress, seeing him to be an apt child, taught him his ABC's; but her husband soon stopped her, saying, "If you teach him to read, he'll soon want to know how to write."

However, some of his white playmates in the streets lent him their spelling books and helped him learn the words. Later, studying the Bible and the newspapers and practicing in secret at night, he learned to write. When this was discovered by his master, he was sent to what was known as a "Negro breaker" to be made a better slave; that is, to be tamed, humbled, taught to be content with slavery, or, in other words, broken. (7)

The man to whom Douglass was sent was named Covey, and he specialized in taking in unruly young slaves for a year or so and "cutting them down to size." Once, when a team of oxen driven by Douglass ran away, he was flogged with ox goads and, as he described it later, "heavy blows flowed freely, and welts were left on my back as large as my little finger. . . . During the first six months I was there, I was whipped either with sticks or with cow skins every week. Aching bones and a sore back were my constant companions." The scars on Frederick's back never went away.

Later, when he was returned to Baltimore, he disguised himself as a sailor, boarded a train and escaped to New York.

Eventually Douglass became famous as a writer and speaker. In a July 4th oration at Rochester, New York, in 1852, he spoke as follows:

What, to the American slave, is your fourth of July? I answer: a day that reveals to him, more than all other days in the year, the gross injustice and cruelty to which he is the constant victim. To him, your celebration is a sham; your boasted liberty, an unholy license; your national greatness, swelling vanity; your sounds of rejoicing are empty and heartless; your denunciation of tyrants brass-fronted impudence; your shouts of liberty and equality, hollow mockery; your prayers and hymns, your sermons and thanksgivings, with all your religious parade and solemnity, are, to him, mere bombast, fraud, deception, impiety and hypocrisy—a thin veil to cover up crimes which would disgrace a nation of savages. . . . You boast of your love of liberty, your superior civilization, and your pure Christianity, while the whole political power of the nation (as embodied in the two great political parties) is solemnly pledged to support and perpetuate the enslavement of three millions of your countrymen. You hurl your anathemas at the crown-headed tyrants of Russia and Austria and pride yourselves on your democratic institutions while you yourselves consent to be the mere tools and bodyguards of the tyrants of Virginia and Carolina. You invite to your shores fugitives of oppression from abroad, honor them with banquets, greet them with ovations, cheer them, toast them, salute them, protect them, and pour out your money to them like water; but the fugitives from your own land you advertise, hunt, arrest, shoot and kill. You glory in your refinement and your universal education; yet you maintain a system as barbarous and dreadful as ever stained the character of a nation—a system begun in avarice, supported in pride, and perpetuated in cruelty. You shed tears over fallen Hungary and make the sad story of her wrongs the theme of your poets, statesmen, and orators till your gallant sons are ready to fly to arms to vindicate her cause against the oppressor; but regard to the tens of thousands of wrongs of the American Negro, you enforce the strictest silence, and would hail him as an enemy of the nation who dares to make those wrongs the subject of public discourse. (8)

Little can be added to the above. We were struck by

the many parallels we can find in today's thinking, even to the mention of fallen Hungary, which some of our local white supremacists compare with conditions in Little Rock, Arkansas, in 1958.

HARVEST OF THE CIVIL WAR

The events leading up to the Civil War, the course and outcome of the war are well known. They did not affect the progress and position of the Negro in America as much as is generally supposed; for, although freedom was hailed as an accomplished fact and the Emancipation Proclamation issued, the Negro remained in economic and psychological bondage.

Many historians feel that, if war had been averted, slavery could have been abolished by peaceful means. As it was, the hatred and resentment in the South resulting from the devastation of war was directed at the usual scapegoat, the Negro. The Yankee was not available to receive the pent-up collective bitterness. The extent of that bitterness was probably not fully known in the North, and most Northerners who were aware of the feeling were at least indifferent. Although they had fought a war ostensibly to secure freedom for the Negro, they seemed to have few qualms in abandoning him to his fate shortly after Appomatox. There were other things close at hand of more immediate interest.

Into the void stepped the Northern politicians. They insisted on projecting the Negro into Southern political life without adequate preparation and without regard for the consequences. The results are best described by a paragraph from Harry Golden's recent book, *For 2¢ Plain,* which reads:

After the Northern politician-faker got through squeezing the last ounce out of it—the playing of the freed slave against the Southern white—he said to the Southerner: "I know it's been tough, boys, but I've got a proposition now. I am ready to leave the Negro dangling in mid-air. Here's the proposition: get your presidential electors to double-cross Democrat Samuel J. Tilden: have them cast their ballots against the popular vote, and put Republican Rutherford B. Hayes in the White House. I know it's a big price to pay, boys, but I'll turn the Negro over to you, lock, stock and barrel, and if you want to let off a little steam, I'll not blame you at all."

This political deal, which in effect ended the Reconstruction Period, was the first of a long series of similar arrangements which take place, even today, between Southern Democrats and Northern Republicans. In such "deals," the Republicans, when needing votes in the Congress for legislation they could not otherwise obtain, can get these votes by sacrificing the Negro. This maneuver has gradually lost its effectiveness because of the growing importance of the Negro vote and the growing awareness of the voting public that nothing has been gained by this senseless confinement of one-tenth of our population to a depressed economic, moral and cultural position.

After the war, and after the Reconstruction Period,

there were few Southerners, black or white, with any degree of security. Many books have been written on the mistakes of the Reconstruction Period; they rarely mention that the Negroes did make slow progress. They held minor political offices, were able to vote, and in most places were gradually establishing themselves, either in agriculture or as domestics in cities.

We often hear that segregation, by law, is traditional in the South and that "Jim Crow" laws, like the poor, have always been with us. Actually, the separate but equal doctrine is not old at all, as time is measured. Nearly all these laws were placed on the books between 1890 and 1910. The reason for them is seldom mentioned.

The Old South is generally pictured as an area of large plantations with stately mansions and, perhaps, hundreds of slaves. On the contrary, out of a population of five million in the South, only about three hundred thousand were slave owners. Most of them owned only from two to five slaves, there being possibly ten thousand planters with the really large plantations having large numbers of slaves.

This same situation existed to a degree within a few years after the War. The same families, with a few newcomers added, pretty much controlled the economy and the politics under the system. The poorer white people were not much better off than the Negro.

In the 1890's a new political party known as the Populists came into prominence and part of their appeal was to the Negro. They tried to show both the Negroes and the poor whites that actually they had much in common, such as the need for schools and job opportunities, the right to vote and the right to participate in organized labor.

The Populists at one time, combining with Negroes and a few radical Republicans, took control and the Negro became the balance of power in Southern politics. This was short-lived. Lulled by dreams of attaining planter status or of rising to foremen, to superintendents, to managers in mills and mines, dirt farmers and poor white laborers listened when they were told their dreams would come to nothing if the Negroes were not "kept in their place." And the poor whites were happy to co-operate.

Even at their lowest ebb, the conservatives had not ceased to fight the coalition of Negroes and whites on matters of mutual interest. Nor had their trusty weapon, racial propaganda, been permitted to rust. Politicians had a field day, each trying to outdo the other in introducing or promising some new piece of "Jim Crow" legislation.

Until 1898, South Carolina had resisted the "Jim Crow" car movement which had swept the South. In that year, the Charleston NEWS and COURIER, the oldest newspaper in the South, fired a final broadside against extremists, as follows: "As we have got on fairly well for a third of a century, including a long period of reconstruction, without such a measure," wrote the editor, "we can probably get on as well hereafter without it." He then called attention to the absurd consequences that could result. "If there must be Jim Crow cars on the railroads, there should be Jim Crow cars on the street railways, also on the passenger boats and Jim Crow eating houses. There should be Jim Crow sections of the jury box and a Jim Crow Bible for colored witnesses to kiss. Perhaps the best plan would be, after all, to take the short cut to the general end . . . by establishing two or three Jim Crow counties and turning them over to our colored citizens for their special and exclusive accommodation."

In trying to reduce his argument to an absurdity, the editor, no doubt, thought he was dealing Jim Crow a telling blow, but there is irony in the fact that what he intended to be absurdity in a short time became a reality. (9) Thus started our segregation laws which, we are told, are part of our "old" Southern tradition.

One of the best explanations for the thinking behind race relations at the turn of the century is found in Lillian Smith's *Killers of the Dream,* in which Mr. Rich White is talking to Mr. Poor White and it reads as follows: (10)

"There's two big jobs that need doing, somebody's got to tend to the living and somebody's got to tend to the nigger. Now, I've learned a few things about making a living and you're too no-count to learn (else you'd be making money same way I make it). But one thing you can learn easy, any white man can, is how to handle the black man. Suppose now you take over the thing you can do and let me take care of the thing I can do best. Anything you want to do to show folks you're boss, you're free to do it. You can run the schools and the churches any way you want to. You can make the customs and set the manners and write the laws (as long as you don't touch my business). You can throw books out of libraries if you don't like what's in them and you can decide pretty much what kind of learning, if any, you want your children to have. If science scares you . . . remember, you don't have to mess around with it. Anyway, it'll tell you things you can't believe and still believe what you believe now, so it's better, maybe, not to take much stock in it.

"If you get restless and don't have a job or your roof leaks, or the children look puny and shoulder blades stick out . . . remember you're a sight better off and better than the black man. . . .

"But if you get nervous sometimes anyway . . and mad with folks and you think it will make you feel a little better to lynch a nigger occasionally, that's OK by me, too; and I'll fix it with the sheriff and the judge and court and our newspapers, so you won't have any trouble afterward, but DON'T EXPECT ME TO COME TO THE LYNCHING, FOR I WON'T BE THERE."

By 1910, nearly all Southern states had a variety of Jim Crow laws. All had contrived to circumvent the 14th and 15th Amendments and the Negro voter had been effectively disenfranchised.

Thus, the majority of the whites sold their birthright for a mess of pottage. It was a birthright that should have entitled them to adequate housing, better jobs, good education and a clear conscience. They sold it for a mess of pottage that included corrupt politics and politicians, low wages, poor schools and lurking doubt as to whether Christianity was really being practiced in the Bible Belt.

Through it all, the Negro survived and endured. He adjusted as he had to in order to stay alive and to eat. Those who refused to conform to the expected pattern invariably learned their lessons the hard way. In looking back, one wonders why the Negro's spirit was not completely crushed. After three centuries of enslavement, a war was fought allegedly to rectify the wrongs done him. But when the war was over, the disillusioned Negro found that those who had promised so much did not really care.

Later, while he adjusted himself as best he could to conditions as they existed, the politician and the business man took over. If a candidate for office felt insecure on the real and important issues of the times, he could always drag out the race issue. And if he preached white supremacy strongly enough, and loudly enough, he could usually win election or re-election, regardless of his qualifications. In their efforts to outdo each other, politicians of the early 1900's were perfectly willing to pit race against race, class against class, religion against religion; and, after working the white electorate up to fever pitch, they would promise any sort of fantastic legislation designed to further humiliate the Negro.

None of this campaign oratory, the state laws passed, or the fears aroused were helpful to the region involved, but race-baiting, to the politician, seemed a sure ticket to election.

The business man could be reasonably sure of cheap labor so long as the white working man was so busy keeping the Negro in line that he hardly had time to consider the benefits of organization. If there was any talk of organization, all management had to do was drop a few hints that there was plenty of Negro labor available at an even cheaper price.

Many of us had uneasy consciences because of all this. But those of us in the South could blame it all on the North, citing cases of individual kindnesses and paternalism to the Negro in the South, overlooking the fact that Negroes were entitled to be treated as men rather than as children. And those in the North told themselves the Negro had more rights there, such as the right to vote and to attend schools of his choice, but forgetting that, after the Negro had sacrificed to put himself through college, jobs were usually denied him because of his color, and that for those who were able to break through the job ceiling and afford a better place to live, better housing was often denied through restrictive covenants, threats of reprisal and economic pressure.

Our attitude toward the Negro through the years has been filled with contradictions and inconsistencies. Though we have prided ourselves on our desire for truth and justice in other fields, we have managed to overlook these attributes where race relations were concerned.

We have sometimes tried to justify our actions on the assumption that certain races are inferior to others. It has never been proved that any races are inherently inferior or superior. Certainly there has been much discussion and disagreement on the subject, but the important point, it seems to us, is WHAT DOES IT MATTER? We do know that in all races the intelligence quotient ranges from zero in some to a genius rating in others. If we took the trouble to make a complete survey, we might find out that the Germans, for example, have a higher IQ, on the average, than the French, that Presbyterians are smarter than Baptists, that men are more intelligent than women. But surely we don't believe that members of any of these groups should be restricted in their endeavors because of such findings. This would not mean that there aren't plenty of Frenchmen smarter than lots of Germans, or that there aren't a lot of brilliant women with stupid husbands.

As Americans, we pride ourselves on recognizing the worth of the individual. We tell ourselves that, in our assimilation of many national, ethnic and religious groups, we have become stronger. But, at the same time, we belittle the accomplishment of the Negro. We criticize the Negro for being inferior, but we save our bitterest criticism for those Negroes obviously not inferior.

We say he tends to be immoral, but we forget that eighty-five per cent of the Negroes in America are of mixed blood and that Negroes couldn't have been over fifty per cent responsible for this fact. We overlook the increase in the divorce rate of white Americans compared with what it was one hundred years ago; while we fail to note that the marital status of the Negro is increasing in stability.

We say we are a religious people; yet we commonly ridicule the religion of the Negro. We complain because the Negro is frequently involved in crimes of violence; but we use every device we can think of to see that he remains bitter because of the job ceiling.

Above all, we make sure he understands he is resented. We put up signs—not *Juden Verboten*, as Hitler did— but *Colored* and *White*. When we have elections in which race is an issue, we run all sorts of inflammatory material in certain of our newspapers, most of which tends to insult or degrade the Negro. Of course, we usually add that we really don't dislike the Negro, provided he stays in his place. This frequently-mentioned "place" has never been clearly defined, but it seems to us it is really a supposedly escape-proof psychic and economic prison. Escape has been difficult, but a surprising number of Negroes have managed it; and the number is growing rapidly. The balance of our story will be devoted largely to those who have "escaped."

GREATNESS HAS NO COLOR

Negroes who have "escaped" have done so only at great sacrifice and against seemingly insurmountable odds, but they not infrequently have had help.

Despite popular misconceptions, there are many in the South who feel that the real Southern traditions are those of friendliness, courtesy, honor and truth and that the tradition of race-caste has been inflated entirely out of proportion. Also, many of us are coming to see that there is nothing sacred about tradition for tradition's sake. There are worthwhile traditions and there are evil traditions. At one time, there was the tradition in New England of burning old women at the stake for witchcraft. Eventually it was decided that this tradition should be dispensed with.

Part of the progress of the Negro has been attained through legal methods. Our system of government, our

Constitution and our laws are based on the premise that all of our people are entitled to equal opportunity and equal justice under the law. Even though laws often have been perverted and justice miscarried where race was a factor, still the Negro recognizes that the basic tenets of our democracy are fundamentally sound and good. Justice, like the mills of the Gods, grinds sure though sometimes exceedingly slow.

We have heard that the Negro is being seduced by Communist ideology. But, as Walter White once said, "It's difficult enough to be black in America without being classified Red, too." Converts to Communism have always been more numerous among oppressed people. To his everlasting credit, the Negro has resisted while others, such as Russians, Chinese and East Europeans, succumbed under less provocation.

Some Negroes have become Communists. Others have tried it, but have been disillusioned. The brilliant Negro author, Richard Wright, who was a card-carrying Communist for several years, renounced it on finding that, while it was true that Communism did not see color, neither did it see the individual—except as a statistic. Those thought to be helpful to the Communist cause were used; those unfriendly or unuseful were discarded or liquidated.

The Negro discovered that in Communism he achieved equality—of a sort; but, in the process, he lost freedom. The majority of the Negro intelligentsia place their faith in America and in our form of government and their faith is beginning to be rewarded.

Possibly more important than the gains made through law are advances made possible by good will and recognition of talent by the American people.

There are certain fields of endeavor which do not lend themselves readily to the artificial barriers erected because of race. We are thinking particularly of the entertainment world, sports, literature, music, the arts and sciences. These are the fields in which the Negro has gained most recognition. It is difficult to "Jim Crow" a magnificent voice, a brilliant writer, or an impressive batting average.

On the other hand, it is difficult to rise to the presidency of a railroad for a man who is not permitted to operate a locomotive, sell tickets, or handle the telegraph key. Starting as a laborer and working up to the presidency was the theme of many a Horatio Alger book. This has been impossible for the Negro because he has not been permitted to take the intermediate steps.

In the period following the Lynch Rule of the early 1900's, few Negroes rose to positions of prominence. Those who did usually found it necessary to make certain concessions to race prejudice. They may not have liked it, but there was little they could do about it.

One such example was Booker T. Washington, founder of Tuskegee Institute, and an advocate of meek cooperation with, and subservience to, the whites, even if it meant loss of dignity and deferment of the hopes for full citizenship. Washington was very popular with white America, both North and South, typifying the Negro as the average white American liked to think of him. His appeal to the good nature and decency of white America seemed good, but the trouble was that *nothing really changed*. All during the period of his influence, lasting until his death in 1915, lynchings continued unabated. In fact, the number of lynchings and acts of violence against the Negro increased. Whether Washington actually had the support of the Negro people is doubtful; although many, no doubt, felt as he did that "half a loaf is better than none."

Others, during the Booker T. Washington era (such as W. E. B. Du Bois), and many more to come later, were not satisfied with Washington's "half a loaf." They refused to be satisfied with anything less than full citizenship—a citizenship other Americans took for granted. They felt they were entitled to the right to obtain the best job they were capable of handling, the right to vote, to run for office, to write, sing and participate in sports on the basis of ability.

Since we are a sports-loving nation, the Negro's spectacular accomplishments in this field naturally impress us. Jackie Robinson was born to a sharecropper family in Georgia in 1919. Later the family moved to California where Jackie starred in football, basketball, track and baseball. In 1947, he signed with the Brooklyn Dodgers, first to crack the color barrier. Since that time, all major league baseball teams have signed Negro players.

As an indication of the terrific impact Negroes have made in the world of sports in the past fifteen years, consider three of our most popular sports.

In major league baseball, Ernie Banks of the Chicago Cubs won the National League's most valuable player award in both 1958 and 1959, with the most runs batted in and the best fielding average. Henry Aaron of the Milwaukee Braves had the League's highest batting average. Willie Mays of the San Francisco Giants, according to reports, is among the highest paid, if not the highest paid, major league baseball players.

In professional football, the leading ground gainer in 1958 and 1959 has been Jimmy Brown of the Cleveland Browns, and Gene Lipscomb was voted outstanding lineman.

In professional basketball, Elgin Baylor was chosen rookie of the year in 1959, and many now rate Wilt Chamberlain as the greatest basketball player of all time.

Most of the Negroes now competing are not supermen, however. They are just young men who finally got the chance to compete; and they are either stars, mediocre, or inferior athletes on about the same percentage basis as their lighter skinned teammates. When we see what they have done in sports, in one generation, given equal opportunity, we begin to see how wrong we have been for denying them equality of opportunity in other fields.

It is a striking fact that often outstanding white athletes from some of the deep South states, where state laws prohibit them from participating in sports events with or against Negroes, are actively sought for Major League teams and end up as teammates of Negroes, with no apparent reluctance. Most athletes are more concerned with the ability of their teammates and with winning than with an "old tradition," which isn't so old after all.

We in Arkansas can take pride not only in our fine Razorback teams but in the fact that, if the opposition happens to have colored players, we play our best, congratulate them if they win, receive their congratulations if we win, and judge opposing players according to their performances.

It is not surprising that few Negroes achieved prominence as authors until recent years. Ability to read and write is a prerequisite in this field, and it was usually considered unwise to permit slaves to become literate. After the Emancipation Proclamation, schooling gradually became available to the Negro. But preparation for anything other than the less remunerative pursuits was either ridiculed or actively discouraged.

Few realize when reading the works of Alexandre Dumas, such as *The Count of Monte Cristo,* that Dumas was a Negro. However, Dumas, although Negro by American racial standards, was completely integrated into his culture and wrote and thought as a Frenchman, not as a Negro.

In 1761, a slave ship docked in Boston and most of the slaves were soon disposed of by auction. However, one girl about twelve years of age seemed too frail to be of value as a slave and was taken to the home of John Wheatley, a well-to-do tailor, and given the name of Phyllis Wheatley. She was never made to feel she was an inferior being and was given all the educational advantages any child of that day and time could obtain. It soon became evident that she had considerable talent for writing and her poems became well known, first in America and later in England. However, she, as Dumas, wrote not as a Negro but as a person not only in, but of, her country.

Phyllis Wheatley was the last Negro author in America to write with a note of optimism for many years. Until recently, all Negro literature has been characterized by an undertone of frustration, bitterness and despair. Among those who achieved recognition were Frederick Douglass, whose autobiography, *Narrative of the Life of*

Frederick Douglass, is an American classic. Booker T. Washington wrote *Up from Slavery.* Paul Laurence Dunbar wrote four novels and many short stories but was best known for his poetry. His career was cut short by his death in 1906 at thirty-four years of age, after an eight-year battle against tuberculosis.

In the early 1920's, there occurred what is sometimes called the Harlem Renaissance, with more and more talented Negroes realizing that in literature they had discovered an avenue of escape from the restrictions imposed on them by their countrymen. One of the most brilliant was W. E. B. Du Bois, educated at Harvard and in Europe, author of *Black Reconstruction, Dark Water* and many others, mostly non-fiction. Others included Frank Yerby, who wrote *The Foxes of Harrow* and *The Vixens,* Willard Motley, author of *Knock on Any Door,* Carl Rowan, author of *Go South to Sorrow,* and William Gardiner Smith, author of *Last of the Conquerors.* Another was Ralph Ellison, who wrote *The Invisible Man.* These represent a small portion, percentagewise, of those who in recent years have been successful in the field of literature. Some of their works have dealt primarily with race problems, but others have ignored race and have written simply as Americans.

To us, the most brilliant and most impelling of the recent Negro authors is Richard Wright, author of the best-seller *Native Son* and many others, including *Black Boy, Uncle Tom's Children* and *White Man, Listen!* His autobiography, *Black Boy,* the shocking story of what it is like to be dark-skinned and talented in America should be required reading for all those having a feeling of superiority or the belief that they have achieved success in life against great odds.

Wright was born of sharecropper parents in Mississippi, who moved to Memphis shortly after his birth. There, because of parental neglect, with both parents working when they could, he was always hungry. At five years of age he would roam the streets, peering under the doors of saloons. He was finally picked up by some of the regular patrons and made to drink for their amusement. By the age of six, he was a confirmed alcoholic. Eventually, this was discovered by an aunt. She took him and his mother to live at Helena, Arkansas, and there, under closer supervision, he forgot his liking for alcohol.

In a short time, his mother suffered a stroke. His father had become an alcoholic and abandoned the family. Until he was twelve, he had never completed a year of uninterrupted schooling. But he was valedictorian of his eighth grade class. This was the end of his formal education.

In 1927, he obtained work at an optical firm in Jackson, Mississippi. He was forced to leave before many months by his white co-workers when they discovered that he hoped to learn the art of grinding lenses instead of remaining on janitor's work.

Eventually, he and his mother returned to Memphis. There he found employment in another optical firm. A white co-worker lent him his library card with the warning that he should keep this indiscretion secret. Wright made trips to the library almost daily, forging notes to the librarian saying: "Give this nigger boy the following books."

His first literary effort was made in the eighth grade. For some reason, he felt he had the ability to write. His first fiction piece was accepted and published by a local

Negro newspaper; but rather than being encouraged to continue to write, he was either ridiculed or told plainly that it would be wiser to desist. Wright tells of his reaction in his book, *Black Boy*:

From no quarter, with the exception of the Negro newspaper editor, had there come a single encouraging word. It was rumored that the principal wanted to know why I had used the word "hell." I felt that I had committed a crime. Had I been conscious of the full extent to which I was pushing against the current of my environment, I would have been frightened altogether out of my attempts at writing. But my reactions were limited to the attitude of the people about me, and I did not speculate or generalize.

I dreamed of writing books, novels, I kept hope alive in me. I knew that I lived in a country in which the aspirations of black people were limited, marked off, yet I felt that I had to go somewhere and do something to redeem my being alive.

I was building up in me a dream which the entire educational system had been rigged to stifle. I was feeling the very thing that the state had spent millions of dollars to make sure that I would never feel. I was becoming aware of the thing that the Jim Crow laws had been drafted and passed to keep out of my consciousness. I was acting on impulses that senators in the nation's capitol had striven to keep out of Negro life.

Later, near the conclusion of his autobiography, Wright

had this to say:

> The white man said he knew "niggers," and I was what the white man called a nigger. Well, the white man had never known me, never known what I thought, what I felt. The white man said that I had a "place" in life. Well, I had never felt my "place" or rather, my deepest instincts had always made me reject the "place" to which the white man had assigned me. It had never occurred to me that I was in any way an inferior being and no word that I had ever heard fall from the lips of a white man had ever really made me doubt the worth of my own humanity. True, I had lied, I had stolen. I had struggled to contain my seething anger. I had fought, and it was, perhaps, a mere accident that I had never killed . . . but in what other ways had the white man allowed me to be natural, to be real, to be myself, except in rejection, rebellion and aggression?

One wonders after reading these words of Richard Wright how many millions of colored men and women have had feelings similar to Wright's, but because they were, as you and I, with no special talents for writing, or medicine or music or baseball, there was no way out; so they continued to express themselves in rejection, rebellion and aggression.

For many years, the Negro in the theater, both on the legitimate stage and in motion pictures, was given few, if any, roles other than the stereotyped buffoon or a servile status. In recent years, however, this policy has undergone gradual change. Nationwide television as well as motion pictures have made us realize that talented Negroes can star in dramas as well as in baseball.

Some of those particularly successful are Dorothy Dandridge and Lena Horne, Harry Belafonte, Sammy Davis, Jr., and Sidney Poitier. Poitier's performance was so outstanding in *The Defiant Ones* that he was a strong contender for the "Best Actor of the Year" Academy Award. He was also distinguished in such movies as *Blackboard Jungle, No Way Out*, and *Something of Value*.

In art, Negroes achieving considerable success include Charles Alston, well-known Brooklyn sculptor and painter, John Rhoden, ranking sculptor among three hundred candidates and recipient of a Fulbright Award, Aaron Douglas and Richmond Barthe, famous sculptor-painters.

The names of Nat "King" Cole, Johnny Mathis, Ella Fitzgerald, Duke Ellington and Sarah Vaughan are well known to those who like popular music, as is the name of W. C. Handy, called "Father of the Blues." Those who prefer the classical enjoy the singing of Marian Anderson and Robert McFerrin of the Metropolitan Opera, or the music of Dr. Clarence Cameron White, world famous violinist.

Negroes who have distinguished themselves in scientific pursuits in recent years include: Dr. Lloyd A. Hall of Chicago, one of the world's top food chemists; Metallurgist James A. Parsons of Ohio, one of the nation's top authorities on rust-resisting iron alloys; Mathematician J. Ernest Wilkins, Jr., University of Chicago, Ph.D. at nineteen, and an atomic energy expert; Ella Tyree, biologist, known for her experiments of injecting atomic materials into animals to determine the effects of radiation on humans; Phillip A. Sellers, researcher, who prepared an anti-cancer compound with radioactive carbon, for a midwestern university, and who has performed experiments with protoactinium, one of the rarest of elements; John Blanton, graduate of Purdue, one of the top men in the field of guided missiles and group leader of rocket turbines for Bell Aircraft Company of Buffalo, New York; Douglas W. Fletcher, engineer and designer of reservoirs, tunnels and pumping stations for the Department of Public Works in Detroit, Michigan. (11)

Many have found their niche in the fields of medicine, rather than the fields of cotton. Some outstanding examples are Dr. Daniel Hale Williams, first to successfully suture the human heart; Dr. Charles E. Drew, first to successfully use blood plasma, and recipient of the Spingarn Award for outstanding achievement in 1944; Dr. Aubre de L. Maynard, widely known New York surgeon and authority on the management of heart wounds; Dr. John E. Mosley, noted cancer specialist of Mt. Sinai Hospital in New York City.

Time and space do not permit the mention of more than a few areas in which the Negro has achieved spectacular successes in recent years; nor do they permit the mention of more than a few individuals in each of the fields mentioned.

In our research, we were amazed to discover the thousands upon thousands who have contributed so much more to our culture than is generally understood, possibly much more than many of us want to understand.

In considering the number of Negroes who have broken the shackles of their environment and gone on to achieve success, we should not forget that in each case they faced more than the customary difficulties confronting all—the long and arduous study required to become a doctor, the long hours of practice necessary to become a professional athlete, the tremendous amount of work, research and education to write a book. These barriers discourage most of us. The Negro has battled the added handicap of the caste system when he needed all his talents and energies to learn what he had to know in his chosen work.

To consider only the successes achieved by outstanding Negroes is to miss a most important point: If they were able to do what they did in spite of the handicaps they endured, how many more might have been on the list if their opportunities had been equal to those of other Americans! Cures might have been discovered for diseases still incurable and discoveries made enabling us to outstrip Russia in the space program.

NEW WAYS FOR AMERICA

Most Negroes, as in the case of the rest of us, are not equipped for the specialized fields mentioned above, but must find a place in industry. The first great migration of the Negro from farm to city and particularly to the great metropolitan centers of the North occurred about the time of the first World War. Large numbers were employed in Chicago in the meat packing industry, in Detroit in automobile factories, and in New York, Philadelphia, St. Louis and other cities in various industries.

However, the birth of new opportunities for the Negro was not without travail. Many were not able to make the transition from the old way of life to the new unscathed; and, although organizations such as the Urban League were of considerable help, new problems often replaced the old. Housing was scarce. It was usually in overcrowded slums and overcharging was the rule.

To add to their woes, Negroes were usually denied membership in labor unions. They were deeply resented by white workers in industry and were often used as strikebreakers in times of industrial strife. Most Negroes newly arrived from the farms and small towns of the South did not understand the intricacies of collective bargaining. To them a job was a job; so they were often used by management as a lever to keep the white workers from getting too far out of line in their demands.

At first the unions went along with management and either barred Negroes from membership or refused to permit their upgrading to the more skilled occupations. Eventually, however, they were forced to the conclusion that it would be necessary to erase the color bar to eliminate a potential source of strikebreaking.

After World War I, and especially during the great depression of the thirties, the Negro became a double victim—both of racial discrimination which resulted in lack of seniority and of the general economic decline which affected all.

As the depression ended and war threatened, the situation changed. Instead of being unneeded, Negro labor was again in great demand and the second great migration took place.

Most of the old employment practices, the restriction of Negroes to the lowest paid, dirtiest and most undesirable jobs, still existed at this time. But many were working to correct these evils. In June, 1941, A. Philip Randolph, Negro labor leader, and others conferred with President Roosevelt, asking for his help. As a result, Executive Order 8802 was issued, creating the Fair Employment Practices Committee. This set a pattern for several states and greatly reduced discrimination in industry. Shortly thereafter, Negroes were employed for the first time as motormen and conductors on the street railways and bus lines in many of our larger cities. Many were upgraded to semi-skilled and skilled jobs in the automobile, steel, meat-packing and other industries.

In 1946, President Truman moved far beyond Franklin Roosevelt on the Civil Rights issue when he established a fifteen-man committee on civil rights and strongly supported fair employment practice laws. The anticipated protests materialized immediately, but Harry Truman stood firm. Many thought his actions might hurt his chances for election in 1948, yet he scored a surprise victory over Tom Dewey.

James Forrestal, as Secretary of the Navy, and W. Stuart Symington, first Secretary of the Air Force, had initiated action during the latter part of World War II to abolish segregation in their branches of the service; and, in 1951, under President Truman, segregation was entirely eliminated from the Armed Forces.

To return to the progress made by the Negro through organized labor, we cannot help but notice many similarities and parallels between the efforts of the laboring man (regardless of color) to improve his position and the efforts of the Negro to improve his. With each group, any indication of a competent organization was violently opposed at first. In each case, the opposition could be depended upon to say, "We were getting along just fine here until these outside agitators came in stirring up trouble." "Everything was nice and peaceful." Or, "We know what's best for our employees (or 'Nigras')."

It probably was "peaceful." . . . But, in the case of the laborer, he could be discharged without regard to length of service to make room for the boss's nephew, worked overtime without additional pay, his just grievances ignored and salary kept at levels lower than required for a decent standard of living. In the case of the Negro, it was also "peaceful," but Negro filling station attendants could be shot for arguing with white customers about the correct amount of change. They could be denied decent housing in the Chicago area and such places as Dearborn, Michigan, denied Pullman accommodations and restricted to sub-standard schooling during this era of peace.

In each case, it could be stated with truth that some organization leaders were more concerned about personal gain than with progress for the group they represented. Each group has, no doubt, made mistakes. In the opposition to each group, there have certainly been sincere men who were kind and good and motivated by high standards of morality, but the fact remains that no one knows the needs and desires of any group of people as well as members of that group. No one will represent them with more integrity than they represent themselves. Refusal or inability of any group to defend themselves, regardless of strenuous efforts to prevent this defense, only results in loss of respect for the group involved.

Members of the dominant (white) group who stoutly

maintain that they are looking out for the best interests of the Negro, and that they will "take care" of him, are no more likely to do so than the company or "dummy" union is to fully represent the laboring man. The basic purpose of company unions is to blunt the effectiveness or the appeal of the bona-fide union. A similar aim to blunt effectiveness is behind the arguments we hear from some whites that they can do the best job of looking after the interests of the Negro.

In comparing the similarities between the difficulties encountered by organized labor and by organizations representing racial minority groups, we are confronted with one inescapable fact. Those areas of our country which have offered the strongest opposition to organized labor have also been most vehement in opposition to organizations representing racial minorities. They refuse to admit either group has any rights not given to them because of benevolence. Union labor is now beginning to be more fully accepted in these areas, but by constant appeal to race prejudice, the working man has been kept from realizing that he has been "used" in much the same way as has the Negro.

In recent years, we have observed that nearly all our large and successful corporations have been willing to meet with representatives of organized labor, and work toward a solution of problems in good faith. Also many of these corporations have followed practices that largely eliminated the need for bargaining.

It also seems obvious that, had the Negro not had many grievances in connection with double standards of justice, no organizations would have been formed to represent him. The Negro, like the rest of us, would prefer to be in a position where organization is not necessary.

THE SUPREME COURT SCHOOL DECISION

Of all the milestones in the legal fight for Negro rights, the most controversial, no doubt, has been the 1954 Supreme Court decision concerning public school segregation. Opinions varied widely. It was hailed by some as the second Emancipation Proclamation. Others expressed shock, resentment and surprise. That it would be resented by some was expected, but it should not have been surprising.

In 1933, a young Negro wanting to study dentistry at the University of North Carolina filed a court suit to obtain this right. A similar suit was filed for admission by Negro students to the University of Maryland in 1935, and in Missouri in 1938. These were followed by many more seeking to enter state supported colleges; and, in nearly every case, the court ruled students could not be denied admission because of race. Also during this same period, suits were filed in connection with denial of service to Negroes in railroad dining cars and Pullman cars. Favorable decisions were rendered to those being discriminated against.

In public education, the schools in the Southern and border states had operated on a segregated basis with facilities supposedly separate, but equal. Few pretended that they were equal. By 1916, the separate but equal theory had resulted in such inequality that seventeen

Southern states were spending $10.30 for the education of each white child, as compared with $2.69 for each colored child. For higher education, $6,429,991 was appropriated for whites; $350,000 for Negroes.

As a result of the favorable court decisions, and as it became increasingly apparent that the separate but equal schools might be separate but gave no indication of ever becoming equal, the next logical step was the decision in connection with public school segregation in which the Supreme Court stated that, in their opinion, segregated schools are inherently unequal.

If it did nothing else, the 1954 decision certainly was a shot in the arm to better Negro schooling in the South. Many new schools were built, teachers' salaries increased and a real effort was made to make these schools equal as well as separate.

There had also been considerable progress in improving schooling for the Negro immediately prior to the 1954 decision because of earlier court orders and in anticipation of the decision that was finally rendered.

Apparently the fact that these increased educational opportunities for Negroes might in the long run defeat the purpose of the avowed racists was not considered. At least, it was not discussed. It probably hasn't occurred to the average white supremacist, but Negro children may be less likely to be taught how to be a carbon copy of Uncle Tom or Aunt Jemima in the all-Negro school than they are in most of our newly integrated schools.

The point is that the more education the Negro receives—integrated or segregated—the more likely he is to want to improve things, to right wrongs, and to make something of himself. This is true of all of us, regardless of color. The only real hope for the strong segregationists would have been, years ago, to have held the line on education for the Negro—either denied it entirely or restricted it to the most rudimentary type.

TROUBLE
AT
LITTLE ROCK

The Supreme Court did not and has not required public schools to integrate except where applications were made for entrance by qualified Negro students. We know this in Little Rock now, but there was a good deal of uncertainty prior to 1957 as to what would be required.

We could have used a positive approach from Washington, but we didn't get it. We could also have used some progressive leadership at the state level, but we didn't get that either.

All we got was the same time-worn bundle of bigotry wrapped in the same old carton of demagoguery with old labels, such as "States' Rights" and "Racial Purity." A few new labels were stuck on the old bundle: "Forced Integration" and "United States Supreme School Board." There was some new doubletalk: "I will reveal where I got my information at the proper time," and "I have it from a very reliable source."

Orval Faubus, even though usually not considered a sincere segregationist, had been in politics long enough to realize that his chances for re-election in the summer of 1958 were not good unless the political climate changed. Unlike the man who once said, "I'd rather be right than be President," he apparently decided he would rather be Governor than right. So he promptly pulled the rug from under the Little Rock School Board, did an about-face and assumed the role of the martyred hero, the defender of States' Rights, and champion of the common man (white, of course).

At frequent intervals, he revealed to the local press, radio and TV, rumors he had heard of diabolical plots against him, and how the foreign press, the local press, the clergy, the School Board, the Parent-Teachers Association and the Chamber of Commerce were all aligned against him.

His special target, though, has been a lone Negro woman and he continues to defend us from her. His ability to stand his ground against her has won him praise from many sources. What an heroic accomplishment!

Because of all this, the students in Little Rock high schools and the people of Little Rock were placed in an extremely difficult position. Although most Little Rock people had not been enthusiastic about public school integration prior to 1957, nevertheless, they were, for the most part, taking it in stride and ready to accept it on the limited basis outlined by former School Superintendent Blossom.

Of course, it is common knowledge now that, given the "green light" by Governor Faubus, extremists soon succeeded in changing these attitudes; and the results are so well known nationally and even internationally that there is no point in re-telling.

Soon, we were told that to treat the few colored kids attending Central High School with kindness or even courtesy was contrary to tradition—ignoring the fact that, as a result of our actions, the real Southern traditions of friendliness and courtesy were being wantonly abandoned.

During the next eighteen months, we reaped the harvest of it all. With the regularity of "Old Faithful" geyser, the Governor issued statements denouncing the Superintendent of Schools, the members of the School Board, the Mayor of Little Rock, the Police Chief, the clergy, the Chamber of Commerce, The Parent-Teachers Association, The Women's Emergency Committee, the STOP Committee, and anyone suggesting a course at the slightest variance with that of the Governor and the radical segregationists.

The few Negro students involved were subject to continual harrassment, name calling, and threats of bodily harm.

Later, a teacher purge was attempted and finally, when this failed, public buildings were dynamited. Those involved in these destructive acts have been apprehended but they only acted as they had been encouraged to believe was right and proper. They have been the scapegoats, but the teachers of this philosophy are still doing business at the same old stands in the State Capitol and the House of Representatives in Washington.

All of these things were done supposedly to preserve what we were told was an old tradition, apparently on the assumption that "the end justifies the means." It is too bad that those involved did not stop to think that, whenever unethical or evil means are necessary to a desired end, then the chances are that the end is also unethical and evil.

As a result of all this, we in Little Rock were the targets of some very bad publicity throughout the nation and the world. Much of this was undeserved; as was shown in the summer of 1959 when the people of Little Rock defied Orval Faubus and his smoothly operating political machine, repudiated the radical segregationists on the School Board and retained those members dedicated to reopening our public schools.

Several other states with attitudes similar to those found in Arkansas, such as Virginia, North Carolina and Oklahoma have adopted varying degrees of school integration unaccompanied by racial incidents in or near the schools. But it should be remembered that, in each of these states, the students, the school boards, the law enforcement agencies and the general public had the support and cooperation of their governors, once it was seen that desegregation would be necessary for public schooling to continue. They were encouraged by their governors to prove their good citizenship. We had to prove ours the hard way.

THIS IS WHAT WE FEEL

So we near the conclusion of our story, the history of the Negro in America. The story of a people maligned as possibly no others have been, a people insistent on becoming part of, as well as merely living in, America, a people who even though ridiculed have often displayed more dignity and spiritual honesty than a lot of the rest of us. A people who have been able to say, even though reviled, "Father forgive them . . . they have come a long way." Whether this is because of or in spite of the white man is not important. Certainly there have been many times when this progress was made in the face of a variety of restrictions and barriers the rest of us can scarcely comprehend.

We have attempted to avoid getting into the usual arguments—the pros and cons of integration and segregation. We have avoided sectionalism as far as possible, too. Racial discrimination and prejudice can be found in all parts of America. Artificial barriers to impede progress of Negroes and other minority groups have been erected both north and south of the Mason-Dixon line. These barriers are beginning to crumble because more and more of us are coming to believe that such barriers are undemocratic, unchristian and unwise.

In our research, we found ninety-eight books on race on the shelves of the public library. It was surprising to discover that, of the ninety-eight books, only two could be considered "anti-Negro." Most of them held a viewpoint at considerable variance with that supposedly held by most Southerners; yet the vast majority of these books were written by native Southerners.

Although school desegregation has occupied our attention lately, the right to integrated schooling is probably not the most important need of the Negro. Breaking through the job ceilings may be far more important. There has been a belief that, if the Negro were to become more prosperous, others would somehow become less prosperous. There is no more logic to this reasoning than what we heard during the depression when labor demanded higher wages and better jobs.

In the early 1930's, it was predicted that labor's demands and various social reforms would lead us to bankruptcy. But when labor's demands were given consideration and the social reforms, such as social security and unemployment compensation, were made effective, the nation (and particularly industry) was never more prosperous. Whereas businessmen in 1929 and 1930 seemed to make a pastime of leaping from skyscraper windows, a few years later when the common man was considerably better off financially the industrialists seldom found time to end it all. They were too busy counting their money. When the average man had money in his pocket, it was easier for the manufacturer to sell him consumer goods, for railroads and bus lines to sell him vacation tours and for contractors to sell him new homes.

So it is with fair employment practices. As we lift the restrictions on the Negro and permit him to improve his financial position by working at more remunerative jobs as fast as he learns new skills, the more prosperous we all become.

In conclusion, it would be well to remember that none of our arguments, ideas or opinions will change what has happened. To us, the Negro's progress has been remarkable, considering the obstacles he has faced that the rest of us have not. His progress has accelerated in recent years. There is no indication that the trend will be reversed. All of us, black and white, North and South, owe it to ourselves to plan and act according to conditions as they are. No one is going to turn back the clock.

White America's reaction to the history of the Negro's struggle, his successes and his refusal to accept less than full citizenship has been varied.

Some would have preferred to keep the caste system, restricting the Negro to fewer employment opportunities, less legal protection and smaller recognition of achievements than are enjoyed by others.

Others feel that progress for the Negro has been much too slow and that the treatment the Negro has received in America has been wrong in nearly every respect.

Our primary reaction as we review the achievements of the Negro in America is an emotion as old as mankind. It's the reaction we felt as small boys when we came upon a fight between the school bully and someone else (invariably smaller) which caused us to exclaim, "Why don't ya pick on someone yer own size?" It's the emotion we felt as we watched a small town high school basketball team upset a big city team in the state tournament.

It's the same feeling that makes us uneasy when two thousand high school kids make it rough on nine other high school kids in Little Rock, or when three hundred families make it rough on one family in Levittown, Pennsylvania, and when one hundred and sixty million Americans make it rough on twenty million other Americans. It's an emotion that "Jim Crow" legislation has been unable to control.

History is filled with accounts of individuals, nations, racial and religious groups who have succeeded against great odds. In spite of humble beginnings, countless cruelties, injustice and persecution, the Christian Church survived and conquered men's hearts.

A small band of colonies in America developed into the greatest nation on earth, even though they were considered little more than barbarians by the ruling classes of England.

Later in America the Southern states, even though in a depressed economic condition for many years, refused to stay down. Today they are challenging the rest of the nation in industrial and economic growth.

These victories were won despite doubts, ridicule and opposition—as victory occurred to the One referred to in the first chapter of Saint John, about two thousand years ago, even though the question was asked, *"Can any good thing come out of Nazareth?"*

All of our research indicates to us that the low status of the Negro in this country is cultural. It is forced upon him. It is not inherent. We feel that the Negro is going to assume full citizenship status in America, and soon.

We feel that, in spite of attempts by many to prevent his complete emancipation, full citizenship will be accomplished because our laws, our Constitution, and what is sometimes referred to as the American creed provide for it.

We feel he will do this with or without the help of the white man, but we would like to help.

NOTES

(1) Moon, Bucklin *Primer for White Folks*. N. Y.: Doubleday, Chapter 1.

(2) Embree, Edwin R. *Brown Americans*. N. Y.: Viking Press, 1943, p. 5.

(3) Embree, Edwin R. *Brown Americans,* p. 18.

(4) Atlanta University, Leaflet no. 19.

(5) Redding, Jay Saunders *They Came in Chains: Americans from Africa*. Philadelphia: Lippincott, 1950.

(6) Carter, Hodding *Winds of Fear*. N. Y.: Farrar & Rinehart, 1944, Foreword.

(7) Hughes, Langston *Famous American Negroes*. N. Y.: Dodd, 1954, p. 27.

(8) Du Bois, W. E. B. *Black Reconstruction*. N. Y.: Harcourt, Brace & Co., 1935, p. 15.

(9) Woodward, C. Vann *The Strange Career of Jim Crow*. N. Y.: Oxford University Press, 1955, p. 50.

(10) Smith, Lillian *Killers of the Dream*. N. Y.: Norton, 1955, p. 174.

(11) Chambers, Lucille A. *America's Tenth Man*. N. Y.: Twayne, 1957.

BIBLIOGRAPHY

Alford, Dale *The Case of the Sleeping People*. Little Rock, Arkansas: 1959.

Armstrong, Orland Kay *Old Massa's People*. Indianapolis: Bobbs-Merrill, 1931.

Ashmore, Harry S. *An Epitaph for Dixie*. N. Y.: Norton, 1958.

Baruch, Dorothy *The Glass House of Prejudice*. N. Y.: Morrow, 1946.

Blossom, Virgil T. *It Has Happened Here*. N. Y.: Harper, 1959.

Butcher, Margaret *The Negro in American Culture*. N. Y.: Knopf, 1956.

Carroll, Joseph Cephas *Slave Insurrections in the United States*. Boston: Chapman & Grimes, 1938.

Dabbs, James McBride *The Southern Heritage*. N. Y.: Knopf, 1959.

Drake, St. Clair and Cayton, Horace R. *Black Metropolis*. N. Y.: Harcourt, Brace, 1945.

Dykeman, Wilma and Stokely, J. *Neither Black Nor White*. N. Y.: Rinehart, 1957.

Fineberg, Solomon Andhil *Punishment Without Crime*. N. Y.: Doubleday, 1949.

Furnas, Joseph C. *Goodbye to Uncle Tom*. N. Y.: W. Sloane, 1956.

Hays, Brooks *A Southern Moderate Speaks*. Chapel Hill, N. C.: University of North Carolina Press, 1959.

Henkle, Henrietta *Let My People Go*. N. Y.: Harper, 1941.

Herskovits, Melville J. *The American Negro*. N. Y.: Knopf, 1928.

Johnson, Charles S. *Into the Mainstream*. Chapel Hill, N. C.: University of North Carolina Press, 1947.

King, Martin Luther *Stride Toward Freedom*. N. Y.: Harper, 1958.

Klineberg, Otto *Characteristics of the American Negro*. N. Y.: Harper, 1944.

Lewis, Hylan *Blackways of Kent*. Chapel Hill, N. C.: University of North Carolina Press, 1955.

McGill, Ralph Emerson *A Church, a School*. N. Y.: Abingdon Press, 1959.

Myrdal, Gunnar *An American Dilemma*. N. Y.: Harper, 1944.

Nelson, William Stuart *Christian Way in Race Relations*. N. Y.: Harper, 1948.

Ottley, Roi *Black Odyssey*. N. Y.: Scribner's, 1948.

Rose, Arnold *The Negro in America*. N. Y.: Harper, 1948.

Rowan, Carl T. *Go South to Sorrow*. N. Y.: Random House, 1957.

Smith, Lillian *Now Is the Time*. N. Y.: Viking Press, 1955.

Sprigle, Ray *In the Land of Jim Crow*. N. Y.: Simon & Schuster, 1949.

Srolé, Leo *The Social System of American Ethnic Groups*. New Haven, Conn.: Yale University Press, 1945.

Sutherland, Robert Lee *Color, Class and Personality*. Washington, D. C.: American Council on Education, 1942.

Warren, Robert Penn *Segregation, The Inner Conflict of the South*. N. Y.: Random House, 1956.

Weaver, Robert *Negro Labor*. N. Y.: Harcourt, Brace, 1946.

White, Walter Francis *How Far the Promised Land*.
N. Y.: Viking Press, 1950.

Woofter, T. J. *Southern Race Progress*. Washington,
D. C.: Public Affairs Press, 1957.